With My
White Eye

Enlightening The Eyes Of Our
Understanding

With My
White Eye

Enlightening The Eyes Of Our
Understanding

Reola B. Moore

Living Water Books

John 7:38

He who believes in me, as the scripture has said,
Out of his heart will flow rivers of living water.

With My
White Eye

Enlightening The Eyes Of Our
Understanding

Reola B. Moore

Living Water Books

John 7:38

He who believes in me, as the scripture has said,
Out of his heart will flow rivers of living water.

Dedication

In Loving Memory of

Fred, Albirdia, Willie, and Ola

This book is dedicated
to all those that I call family-
especially Darius, Bree, Justice, and Fredrick,
who happen to call me Mom.

"

As we abide in Christ, and He abides in us, we take on His character. Having the mind of Christ, we see as He does...No longer confined to what we see of our own accord; we are enlarged to see what God sees in us, through us, and for us."

REOLA B. MOORE

Table Of Contents

Chapter Six

Preface

With My White Eye

With my second set of children- yes, there was the first set of two, and one decade later, a second set of two, I decided to do things a little differently. So, instead of reading them bedtime stories all the time, beginning at pre-kindergarten age, I challenged them to tell me stories. They were allowed to formulate stories from whatever resources they found. This could include thoughts from their favorite household decorations and furniture, car ride adventures, school experiences, and even a combination of stories that they had been told before.

There was no requirement of sensibility or length. It was only to teach them how to articulate their thoughts in complete sentences and to be able to connect ideas in sequential order. My youngest son had a healthy appetite, so we were not surprised that all (and I do mean *all*) of his stories had some reference to food. The one story that sticks out in my mind is the one about the tiger that got lost in the woods who became so hungry that he ate his own stripes! Wow!

This reinforced his earlier declaration that I was not putting enough food in his lunchbox and alerted me to his resourcefulness and creative imagination. A few days later, the family was gathered around the dinner table. My daughter attempted to sneak some food from this particular son's plate while he was distracted by talking to me. Without turning his head to face her, he calmly stated,

> *"I know you think I didn't see you but I saw you with my white eye!"*

Of course, he was talking about his peripheral vision. We laughed to tears. As I thought about his comment, I was mesmerized by how our lives are processed through tunnel vision, when there is a galaxy of options accessible through our peripheral.

We miss many promises from The One Who Cannot Lie (God) because we lack the discipline for spiritual vision. Therefore, we live beneath our privileges because we never tap into the authority that God has given us, only being satiated with what is given to us and what is audible and tangible in propinquity.

I am grateful to have expanded my sight. Although this book captures my journey, I admonish each reader to read with self-reflection. Then, prayerfully delve into the pages with the intention of increasing your spiritual sight.

God is omniscient, omnipotent, and omnipresent; therefore, his expanded view is peripherally inclusive.

Reola B. Moore

Chapter One

God's Empathy
Breathed Within Me

From early childhood, I was a self-proclaimed advocate for the underdog. I hated to see people in lack.

I cringed at innocent people being misrepresented or under-represented. I felt the burden of those enduring persecution and bullying. In my eyes, these were the "least ones" that Jesus referred to, and one of the most dangerous and distinctive self-inflicted dooms was to perform an act against one of them…

… the ones who may not have had enough money for the school lunch.

… the ones who wore clothes to school that were possibly worn previously in the same week, or even worse, had been worn by a sibling who attended the same school,

… the ones who were consistently the last chosen to be on a team for any sporting activity,

… the ones who thought that it was customary to eat alone- either because they were not "cool" enough or because they did not share the scent of fresh spring.

These were the children I was instinctively drawn to as if I could make their world a better place. Not knowing the magnitude of the empathy God had allowed me to possess, I felt their pain as if I had been the target of the misfortunes. I guess that whatever comes from the heart does reach another heart because they always let me enter their world. My motives were never questioned, and my responses were never doubted. The interaction among us caused Proverbs 18:24 to come alive between us.

> *Prov 18:24 (NKJV) A man who has friends must himself be friendly, but there is a friend who sticks closer than a brother.*

I had unique living arrangements during my elementary school years. My maternal grandfather worked during the second shift, which was 3:00 p.m. – 11:00 p.m. During the school week, I stayed at my grandparents' home to prevent my grandmother from being home alone at nightfall and was home with my parents and siblings on the weekends. So, when the extended family met to have Sunday dinner at my grandparents' home, that was my signal to transition into my school week arrangement.

I stayed close to my grandmother and learned a lot of things. She was the only person I knew (whether in a licensed beauty salon or at home) who could hot press someone's hair and make that style last for a full two weeks- without a retouch. Unfortunately, I never learned the art of using the hot comb effectively. In fact, several years later, I attempted to give my older brother a blow-out hairstyle and did not know how to gauge the temperature of the pressing comb after it was removed from the fire.

A little bit of sizzle... a whole lot of smoke... and an "uh-oh" from me, and he had an instant side pocket that any pool hustler would have loved. I burned a hole in his afro, and it was quite some time before that hair grew back. He blames me to this day for his early balding! What I did learn is how to hold your ear when you are on the receiving end of the pressing so that what happened to my brother's hair does not happen to your skin.

It is not commonplace to experience quality time with grandparents in the 21st Century, but my youth was invigorated with wisdom from grandparents, aunts, uncles, and a plethora of older relatives. From my grandmother, I gained culinary, sewing, domestic, and hospitality traits. Moreover, time spent with my grandfather was not without its foundational principles and life lessons. Among them are my ability to manicure a lawn and my compulsion to extend a helping hand.

My grandfather shared a lot-sized garden with one of his good friends, who happened to be a nearby neighbor. They, and certainly their grandchildren during school breaks and weekends, worked many hours pulling weeds, tilling the ground, planting seeds, watering the rows, and gathering the harvest. There is nothing like fresh produce, and there is nothing like reaping the benefits of your labor. However, there were times when it was not so fun to be out there working in the sun, and after the tedious task of gathering all the food, I couldn't believe that these two elderly gentlemen gave away so much of it. What? Are they kidding? Are they just going to give this food away that *we* had to work so hard to get? My mind would spin in disbelief.

After I was forced to spend some Saturday afternoons shelling and bagging peas (clearly noted to be time with my parents, where games of kickball awaited me), were they seriously going to give some of the bags away? Who does that? Here was yet another principle from God coming into full view.

1 John 3:17 (NKJV) But whoever has this
world's goods, and sees his brother in need,
and shuts up his heart from him, how does the
love of God abide in him?

My grandmother, amongst a plethora of other titles, was also an excellent cook. To add insult to (my) injury, she would labor over 5-course meals, only to extend a verbal dining invitation to several people throughout the day. First, there was the neighbor who stopped by to borrow a cup of sugar. Then there was the relative who just stopped by to check on the family but happened to be accompanied by two or three of her children. Moreover, there were distant neighbors, friends of my cousins (of whom my grandparents were guardians), and some of our church members who passed by my grandparents' house during their travels.

You could hear my grandmother's response to their greeting, "Hey there! I have cooked. You'd better come on in and get you some!" You would have thought that after all those guests, there would not have been enough for our family to eat, but it was. As if she was modeling Jesus's gesture at the feeding of the multitude, she blessed what she cooked, and there was always plenty. Most times, there were leftovers. It was not until much later in life that I realized that many of the fresh garden food recipients were widows or those who had found themselves in situations with a sudden loss of income. Many of those to whom my grandmother offered a meal had families with several children and were experiencing some form of lack. Because I now know the principle of sowing and reaping, I am sure that God sustained our family because my grandparents' acts were sown in love. A rather significant memory, in hindsight, is my grandmother's role as a confidant.

Being the family disciplinarian, she had a sturdy list of "Don'ts," for which she had an intolerance. This included fighting, disrespecting elders, and speaking ill of others. Yet, remarkably, I never heard her gossip. Undoubtedly, she must have been a good listener because I was excused from her presence when countless people from several occupations, age groups, and social backgrounds engaged her listening ear to share their issues of life. What stood out to me is that

21

many of them often came- even if they had to approach in secret as Nicodemus did with Jesus, and not once did I ever hear anyone accuse her of revealing a conversation.

> *Prov 17:9 (NKJV) He who covers a transgression seeks love, but he who repeats a matter separates friends.*

So, I realized early in life that being confidential in matters was a staple for building trust in relationships, and I embraced it. It proved to be a significant part of every relationship in my life- church, work, college, and even my role as a rescuer in elementary school.

Once I was cognizant of this foundation, I realized that recurrent pattern in my mother. Until the day that she transitioned from this life, she fostered an environment that encouraged people to share their deepest feelings without fear of repercussions or judgment. So, I was given the gift of confidentiality in real-time wrapping.

Chapter Two

Can a Hog See His Own Behind?

My father was well-known for his epigrams. However, one of the most memorable quips was uttered any time his response to one of our questions would be negative.

May I spend the night somewhere?

May I drive your car?

His brows would parallel park, his voice would climb a musical scale, and with a sarcastic purse of the lips, one would hear, "Can a hog see his own behind?". Of course, as a small child, one could only assume that the answer to this rhetorical question was "No!" as its presentation was equated with my father's decision of denial. However, I must say that I always wanted to see an older model Mercury vehicle and inspect its wheels and hubcaps because my father's answer for "No" was the aforementioned quip- except for when it came to money! At that request, he became animated; then there was a plea to not ask for money, as it put tears in his eyes as big as Mercury hubcaps!

Although the hog reference was rhetorical, it only took one family member to think outside of the box and accept the challenge to find the answer. It happened to be my eldest child. Living in Razorback Country, there was a plethora of hog memorabilia in our home, such as an ashtray made in high school Industrial Arts class, razorback paperweights, and a hog bobble-head made of two connecting pieces. I imagine that my son heard the hog response one time too many and decided to determine the answer. He made a far-fetched request of my father, and by the time that my father was poised for his typical response, my son had disconnected the bobble-head, turned the hog's head around in his right hand to get a good view of his body (including his rotisserie rear) in his left.

He then replied, "Oh, yes, he can!". My father was so outdone that he gave in to his grandson's request, and I do not ever remember him using that epigram again. However, he was amused at the presentation and impressed with my son's analytical process.

As an adult, I frequently reflect on that saying, as well as the amusing image. If the hog cannot see his rear, why can't he? Is it because of his anatomical design and/or weight, lack of effort, or tunnel vision? In all fairness, it is due to a combination of each, but in human comparison, the answer is weighted more in our vision. Why are we so focused on what we want, when we want it, and how we want it? As with a cleaned hog succumbing to a mudhole, why do we return to the weak and beggarly things?

... the filthy conversations?

... the muddy attitudes?

…the toxic associates and environments?

Like the mud to the hog, the answer is that those things are comfortable and pleasing to the flesh. But unfortunately, it is the same reason our peripheral vision is diminished, not to be moved with compassion for others.

> *Prov 16:2 (KJV) All the ways of a man are clean in his eye, but the Lord weigheth the spirits.*

Chapter Three

Are You Cutting The Right Thing Down?

My parents were slightly aged when I was born, which caused me to live somewhat sheltered as a child. Thus, I needed an experience as a young adult to help me mature and develop some independence. I bypassed a full scholarship to a university in my state to accept a partial scholarship in a neighboring state. My reasoning for this was that this school was far enough away from my home that my parents would not attempt to visit every weekend, but close enough that they could arrive there in a short period of time if the need had arisen. This campus and dorm experience is one that I would not trade for anything because I formed bonds and gained lifelong friends that I call the T-Connection.

My roommate, who has maintained sisterhood with me for almost 40 years, made my nightlife in the dorm interesting because she was an excellent cook. So, I was not sure if our regular evening visitors' motives were to receive tutoring from me or a plate from her. She attended this university via an athletic scholarship and (I might add) was an outstanding basketball player. Before the strenuous basketball season got underway, she took the opportunity to return home for weekend visits with her family. I then discovered that I had a crew of big brothers from both the football and basketball teams.

They took it upon themselves to make me aware of the campus meal schedule by arriving in groups to escort me to the cafeteria for weekend breakfast, lunch, and dinner. They instructed and accompanied me on where to go on campus, gave strong opinions on what I could do and with whom I could do it, and to this day, remain somewhat protective of me.

I made the naïve assumption that everyone attending college was my approximate age and had similar home experiences to mine. Boy, was I amazed to know that some people either transferred to this institution from a junior college or were there to obtain advanced degrees and that the numbers that defined their ages qualified them to be legal adults! Not all students enjoyed the latitude of starting a college education immediately after completing high school. Imagine my surprise when I discovered that some students did not have the privilege of traveling to see their families on the weekends or during summer break because a trip home might take 24 hours of travel time and cost thousands of dollars! Yes, I forged lasting international friendships, as well.

My college campus experience taught me many things, some of which to replicate and some of which to eschew.

I encountered people from all walks of life daily, and the greatest thing I learned is that people can only respond from their milieu. Whatever factors are included in their rearing environment help to establish their character. From the depths of their character flow their actions, reactions, and perspectives. So, a fair judgment of a person's actions and responses can only be determined after fully understanding their core.

Too often, we judge others' appearance or actions without attempting to understand how they got there. I remember feeling the hurt of a young lady who was chastised (by someone who felt comfortable enough to address her) for cutting her hair. It was the scorner's opinion that the style was too short and that it projected a male silhouette. The elder woman went on and on about the former state of the beauty of the young lady's hair.

Finally, embarrassed and hurt, the young lady revealed that chemotherapy treatment for her cancer diagnosis caused her baldness.

In that moment of stunned silence, I could only reflect on the poison attributed to the tongue. Those sharp words of reprimand could not be retracted, and the elder- now in a state of shame- could not fathom a way to repair the damage.

1 Sam 16:7(NKJV) For the Lord does not see as man sees; for man looks at the outward appearance, but the Lord looks at the heart.

The faults and misdirection's of others are so apparent that they become targets for judgment in the flesh. However, it would benefit us to remember that while we may not be guilty of the communication that has caught our condemnatory eye, we are not blameless of some action, or even some thought, which has caused us to be undeserving of God's glory. Oh, that gnat diet! We easily swallow the camel and gag on the gnat of our own lives.

Romans 3:23 KJV For all have sinned and come short of the glory of God.

Understanding, or at least becoming cognizant of others' vulnerability to temptation, should be a compass for directing our prayers for them.

As we tend to be a product of our environment, one should not be surprised when another's dietary habits, profane communications, or risky behaviors are modeled outside of the environment. In this sense, I have learned to target the person's desires, tastes, and gratification in my authoritative prayer for them. I have found that it takes an ax to the root of the action.

> *Who can have compassion on the ignorant, and*
> *on them that are out of the way; for that he*
> *himself also is compassed with infirmity.*
> *Heb 5:2 KJV*

There is a colossal difference between trying on someone's shoes and actively wearing them. My empathy for the underdogs was highlighted by my attempt to understand their journey to put myself in their shoes. There is an idiom that admonishes, "Before you judge a man, walk a mile in his shoes." Even when inheriting a used pair of shoes, one might not realize that the direction of stride and the degree of wear is also inherited. My feet are narrow, and when I have been given a pair of shoes that has been even slightly worn,

I cannot manage an optimal fit. Trying to wear my son's size 15 shoes or my grandson's size 3- well, let us just say that it would not be a pretty picture!

However, all too often, that is what happens when we do not learn to cast burdens on God. Instead, we try to carry what God intended to be brought to him. In the mode of compassion, we take on others' issues and become weighted down with them. The ensuing disfigurement renders us unable or unwilling to bear the infirmities of the weak in the future.

> *1 Pet 5:7 (KJV) Casting all your care upon him; for He careth for you.*

God's view of us compared to how we see ourselves is vaster than our natural peripheral view is from our center of gaze.

Reola B. Moore

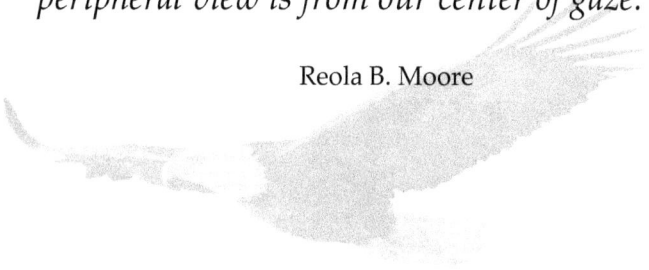

Chapter Four

Do You See What I See?

My life took an abrupt pause while in the middle of writing this book, as my mother was diagnosed with and succumbed to cancer. One of my mother's favorite songs was *Too Close to the Mirror,* performed by Eddie Ruth Bradford. The psalmist sentiments being too close or too connected to the natural, to see herself as God does. God's timing, ways, and thoughts towards us are as far as the heavens are from the earth. Compared to how we see ourselves, God's view of us is vaster than our natural peripheral view is from our center of gaze. We must take note of the progression that frames why we do what we do. Our thoughts define our actions and interactions. Our thoughts are shaped by what we experience, what we see, and what we hear.

Thus, we conclude that the eyes are the windows to the soul. We are then categorized by perception. Some see the glass half-empty, while others see it half-full. If a person's environment has been that of abuse, neglect, demeaning overtures, and the like, he or she is prone to exhibit and accept actions associated with low self-esteem. They will likely settle for that present state of being. Contrarily, one nurtured with a robust support system, afforded development opportunities and echoes of encouragement, tends to pursue further development, accepts challenges, and exhibits confidence and self-empowerment.

God is omniscient, omnipotent, and omnipresent; therefore, his expanded view is peripherally inclusive. The balance in accepting God's view of us is one of acknowledging that it is unmerited, yet graciously afforded; it is empowering, yet humbling. God sees our present state, but accepts our future being, so it is defining. Through the blood of Jesus, He sees us as He ordained us to be. God's view magnifies psalmist

Donald Lawrence's exclamation of us being *spiritual* beings having a natural experience.

> *Eph 2:13 KJV But now in Christ Jesus, ye who sometimes were far off are made nigh by the blood of Christ.*

I am not altogether sure that my mother is not owed some residual income for the emergence of the WWJD movement. She was one of the greatest proponents of measuring one's proposed actions against those exhibited by Jesus. Many times, after making declarations to her about what I intended to do or say, she would sweetly respond, "Now, think. What would Jesus do?" What a sobering re-direction! In fact, my mother modeled the Golden Rule, and she never allowed us to adopt a Bronze or Silver one. It did not matter the circumstance. If we presented with an injury- she would not accept the possibility of it being intentionally caused. If we experienced a loss or theft- surely someone must have needed the item more than the victim. She was determined to see the inherent "good" in everyone.

> *Psalm 32:2 KJV Blessed is the man unto whom*
> *the Lord imputeth not iniquity, and in whose*
> *Spirit, there is no guile.*

With the calmest of spirits, she affirmed that she did not hang out with Anxiety and that Sadness was not a close neighbor. Any time either of these culprits attempted to pull her from God's intended place, she advised that she would simply reach inside herself and pull out joy or peace or any attribute of the fruit of the Spirit that was needed. Of course, there is a principle of harvest applied here. If there had been no seed of God's Word planted and cultivated within her, the produce of the fruit of the Spirit would not have developed; and, therefore, would not have been available for harvest at the time of need.

> *Gal 5:22-23 (KJV) But the fruit of the Spirit is*
> *love, joy, peace, longsuffering, gentleness,*
> *goodness, faith, meekness, temperance: against*
> *such there is no law.*

Unfortunately, my mother could never carry a tune in a bucket, not even one with a liner and reinforced handles attached. But she followed the command of the

38

Psalmist David to 'make a joyful noise unto the Lord', and anyone that had the pleasure of knowing her can attest that she 'served the Lord with gladness.' Instead of singing, she spoke the lyrics of certain hymns in poetic verse.

As she aged, she began to forget the news that she saved up to share with family members and to misplace small items in the house. She shared with me that she did not believe in worrying. "All you have to do," she confidently exclaimed, "is ask God to help you." With that, she would intensely and, in a melody of several keys, sing, "Oh, Lord, I need you to help me!" A short time later, she would remember the person's name she was pondering or recollect where the missing item lay. She swore by it. Oh, how great a faith! I alluded to the fact that there is some discipline involved in spiritual sight. The discipline includes reading the Word of God, believing it, applying it, and clinging to it. The Bible commands the just person to live by and walk by faith-not by sight.

2 Cor 5:7 (KJV)
For we walk by faith; not by sight.

This means you must be able to go beyond what you see with your baby blue or soft brown eyes and begin to see people and things with your white eye- now evidenced as your *spiritual* eye. Using the spiritual eye means seeing as God sees.

So then, we hate the sin, but not the sinner. The sinner is recognized as a soul to whom God has extended an invitation to be saved. The natural eye sees a person's present, while the spiritual eye sees the person's potential. The natural eye sees and exploits differences in race, socio-economic status, gender, and the like. The spiritual eye operates with no respect of person.

Chapter Five

Night Vision

Most people would agree that, unless you are an innately nocturnal being, there is a certain degree of difficulty viewing objects in the absence of light. Sometimes, the light illuminates the object directly; at other times, light clearly reveals the direction in which the object is located. I am reminded of David when he declared the Word of God to be a lamp unto his feet and a light unto his path. Only with God's Word are we able to live out the plan of God for our lives, the place of His "expected end." To fully execute His plan, believers must see things, circumstances, and people (including themselves) as God sees them.

I would have readily declared that experiencing my mother's death was the darkest hour of my life.

After all, my honored position in the family was as the only daughter to whom she had given birth. Additionally, I had a cuisine connection: providing her a choice of burgers or fish on Fridays (which replicated her father's tradition), dining at a different restaurant *every* Sunday, and for 25 years, preparing every major holiday meal from Easter to Christmas.

Unquestionably, there was a deep and sudden void in my life. In retrospect, I had experienced similar devastation some 15 years prior, with the loss of my father, in the middle of a pregnancy, while learning a new job and believing God for his healing. Ding, ding, ding. We have a tie! Wait a minute; there is an upset! What could possibly weigh in heavier than these two losses? Right in the middle of settling estate affairs and getting my life back on track (three months after starting a new career and four days before I was scheduled to travel across the country for a work conference), one of my children became incarcerated!

I was cognizant of the fact that the enemy will challenge a believer at the point of an expressed declaration, and I had had the opportunity to address my local congregation four days prior to this incident. I expected the enemy to come- but not this way. I cried out to God, prayed, quoted scriptures, and even joined in faith with prayer partners, and things got worse. THAT is when I realized my darkest hour. So, I had to ask myself, "Do you believe the Word that you proclaimed?" After unapologetically confirming that I believed, I began to really take a stand on the Promises of God.

> *Eph 6:13 (KJV) Wherefore take unto you the whole armor of God, that ye may be able to stand in the evil day, and having done all, to stand.*

So came the questions: If you call me, and I do not answer like you are used to me answering, will you still trust that I heard and will answer your prayer? What if the situation does not align with what you are declaring; will you trust that I am working it out for your good- just because you are called according to my purpose? And, what if no one believes like you do (family, friends and legal included); will you root yourself in knowing that my plans for you include peace and bringing you to an expected end? Knowing that I could trust God during this time meant having night vision or seeing in my darkest hour. In hindsight, this was an easy task because God is Light.

If unlike Peter, we keep our eyes on Him while we are going through, we will always come through victoriously! God never promised us that we would not have difficulties in life. In fact, as a Believer, we are targeted for persecution because of the Word of God. Sometimes we must face the challenge of things not looking or sounding favorable so that we can choose to believe the report of the Lord, which is in direct contrast to what we are experiencing. When we see it God's way, we know that we have victory before a battle even begins.

> *1 John 5:4(KJV) For whatsoever is born of God overcometh the world: and this is the victory that overcometh the world, even our faith.*

As we examine the fullness of our purpose, we find that we are all commissioned as intercessors to some degree. Christ's ascension after His resurrection placed Him at the right hand of Father God. He is there now, constantly interceding for you and me, which makes Him the ultimate intercessor. Because of this, all Christian prayer becomes intercession since it is offered to God through and by Christ. Intercession is, by definition, intervening on behalf of someone else.

It is not enough to know the plight of others, but intervening is praying, and when possible, taking action because of it- despite it- in the midst of it, as you are compelled to do so. Moreover, as Kingdom citizens, we have been given dominion and authority in the earth. From a pure and selfless heart comes the burden of Kingdom harvest and the privilege of calling things that are not as though they were. We become the gap between God and the ones who have ignited the burden in our hearts, and while we are interceding for others, Jesus is still interceding for us.

Moreover, the Holy Spirit is making intercession for us, as well. Thus, it is a win-win situation.

I am persuaded that God allows us to see things because of the action that will follow. There are those who feel the burden and see the plight of others and take on the persona of scoffing, ridiculing, blaming, or ignoring. If we, as believers, have a High Priest who is not void of compassion, then should not the world have the same (on Earth as it is in Heaven)?

We are the royal priesthood on earth, and as such, should reflect the being of our High Priest. Therefore, we should be moved with compassion; (1) because we have the authority and power to do so and (2) because we are connected to the breakthrough.

1 Pet 3: 8-9 (KJV) Finally, be ye all of one mind, having compassion one of another, love as brethren, be pitiful, be courteous: Not rendering evil for evil, or railing for railing: but contrariwise blessing; knowing that ye are thereunto called, that ye should inherit a blessing.

So, my life comes together. It was not by accident that my grandmother cooked extra meals or that my grandfather harvested an oversized garden. They felt the burden, and in addition to prayer, acted according to the need. It was not a coincidence that I was led to befriend the underdog or that I frequently had extra lunch to share. God will not ask you to take from someone else's hand, but like with Moses, He asks the question, "What's in your hand?"

Life and death are in the power of the tongue. We are commissioned to build the Kingdom of God by speaking and causing life. It takes nothing from us to go from "I told you so" to "I told the storm." When encountering a person acting out of character- whether because of mental illness, rebellion, or influence of foreign substance- God is pleased when you call a "sound mind" back to the afflicted. It has been said that actions speak louder than words. What if both your actions and your words are in line with the Word of God? This must be a symphony.

God sees all and knows all. He uses many symbols in the Bible to show us the indescribable and incomprehensible workings of Himself. Our faith transforms our eyes to see as He sees.

Reola B. Moore

Chapter Six

Using Your White Eye May Cause A Black Eye

The one statement that resounds from my very first college accounting course is "everything has to balance." I had trouble with accounting terminology until my aged professor broke it down in laymen's terms. For example, if you purchase an item from your checking account (back then, he meant actual physical checks), you must remember to deduct that amount in your ledger to show an accurate balance. We see it in the law of gravity: what goes up must come down. We see it in the Word of God: whatsoever a man soweth, that shall he also reap. As a child, I mimicked my grandmother when she versed it- daily- in a stern tone,

49

but she said it like this "what you do, comes back to you."

In general, Christians tend to ask God to increase their faith. Seldom is it recognized, but to be increased, that measure of faith must be tried. We do not realize that we are asking God to send us a trial. The balance is that you are building spiritual muscles during the trial, increasing a prayer life, learning to hear God, and getting to know Him better. This makes you a formidable force for the next trial. There is a spiritual balance in seeing as God sees that is not readily discussed, one that makes you a target of the enemy.

Earlier, I discussed the unction to intercede deriving from what is seen physically, the burden felt, and compassion adopted regarding the needs of others (including those who are too weary to pray for themselves), and the empathy drawn from the actions of individuals and groups who have no idea that they are in need of prayer. Extra! Extra! This includes your enemies. It brings to mind Jesus's plea of intercession "Father, forgive them, for they know not what they do."

Another aspect of intercession is knowing what has been demonically assigned to happen and taking authority over it to cancel it. This often comes in dreams and visions. Every time you rebuke sickness, disease, marital disengagement, addiction, and especially death from overtaking a soul, you may be adding to God's Kingdom, but you are also subtracting from the kingdom of the enemy. Trust me, Satan does not take it lightly, and at this point, you might as well be wearing a bull's eye target. The good thing is that God is always on your side. If you have made it to the point of having rebuking authority, you have been tested and tried in the faith and are mature enough to allow God to fight your battles.

> *Isaiah 54:17(KJV) No weapon that*
> *is formed against thee shall prosper; and every*
> *tongue that shall rise against thee in judgment*
> *thou shalt condemn. This is the heritage of the*
> *servants of the Lord, and their righteousness is*
> *of me, saith the Lord.*

Unlike my childhood, I had begun to intercede purposefully, but I was unaware of this "balance" revelation. In the Word of God, it was unfathomable to Job's wife and friends that he did not commit an offense to God because his trials were so severe. However, it turns out that he was chosen to be tested because of his upright position with God. No, I am not comparing myself to Job. But, after a series of life-threatening events, I did not need a spouse or friends to question me. Instead, I started evaluating myself. It was not until a year into this turmoil that I was reminded of what I had done. "Didn't you start writing that book?" She asked. I had stirred up the enemy's camp by exposing some of his tactics! Although Jesus gave us authority over all devils, many believers do not exercise it, mainly because they are unaware that they have it.

So, the first blow to satan is recognizing who we are and whose we are. Unfortunately, not everyone handles being given authority well.

> *Proverbs 29:2 (KJV) When the righteous are in*
> *authority, the people rejoice: but when the*
> *wicked beareth rule, the people mourn.*

A second blow comes from being sober-minded and staying in a Holy place to execute righteous authority fully. This involves renewing our minds daily with the Word of God.

> *1 Peter 4:1 KJV Forasmuch then as Christ hath*
> *suffered for us in the flesh, arm yourselves*
> *likewise with the same mind: for he that hath*
> *suffered in the flesh hath ceased from sin.*

The thief comes to steal, kill, and destroy. This scripture is quoted haphazardly, but it is an imminent reality. There are many things that the enemy wants to steal and destroy from the believer, such as your faith, your joy, your peace, your prayer time, and your character; anything to turn your focus from the promises of God. I came to know that he wants to physically KILL you. Why, you might ask? The most prominent reason is that without your physical and spiritual presence, without your rebuking authority to his reign, there is one less threat to his kingdom. That is one less person tearing his kingdom down and one less person snatching a soul from the grips of hell.

I came to know this because I experienced it. Just from penning this book, my family received a black eye. One of my children was shot while walking home. What should have shattered his leg, went in, bypassed every muscle and tendon, and came out cleanly on the other side. ("...lo I am with you always." Matthew 28:20.) Our residence was the target of a drive-by shooting- not once, but twice. The first time, bullets entered at midnight, inches from a bedside. After submitting the manuscript to the publisher, the second attack happened like a scene from the *Wild Wild West*. I was afforded the opportunity to work remotely that day. I felt an unction to purchase lunch. This stands out to me because it was pressing, and the timing was about 1 ½ hours before I normally break for lunch. During my thirty-minute absence, our residence was riddled with forty rounds of rifle-styled bullets. The enemy literally wanted to kill me. My saving grace is that I plead the blood of Jesus over our lives daily. This I know that I know that I know, and might ought to manufacture a wardrobe depicting: THE BLOOD STILL WORKS!

Psalm 118:17 KJV I shall not die, but live, and declare the works of the Lord.

When receiving a physical black eye- whether by accidental or intentional injury- there is a period of healing. Vessels will retract, muscles will calm, swelling will cease, sight will be regained, and the victim will gain a sensitivity to the possibility of this type of injury recurring. Likewise, spiritually, we are persecuted for the Word's sake, but it is the same Word that brings our victory.

We are not ignorant of the enemy's devices. One of his most popular tactics is manipulating the mind. He intently attempts to cause us to shift focus from God's Promises to our problems. But the Promises of God are Yes and Amen! I admonish believers to keep the focus on them. If He says He has plans of good to bring us to an expected end, that is what we need to expect.

Philippians(KJV) Being confident of this very thing, that he which hath begun a good work in you will perform it until the day of Jesus Christ.

Conclusion

Whether our ability to see passes a standard eye exam or we need to take advantage of prescription eyewear or lenses, God gives each of us an opportunity to increase our spiritual vision to perfection. The greatest commandment issued by God directs us to "love God with all of our hearts, all of our minds, and all of our souls; and subsequently, to love our neighbors as ourselves." This poses an intensifying problem if the love is faltering. You cannot love another if you do not know how to love yourself genuinely (yea, not vanity, but agape epitomized), and I dare say that you will fail in loving yourself if you have not fallen in love with the Creator God. Until we see ourselves as Yahweh sees us- fearfully and wonderfully made; His workmanship whom He called "good and very good"; one who bears His image and houses His Spirit- we will not see others in that same light. At our best, we are undeserving of

God's goodness. Yet, He extends Grace, sufficient unto our needs. In our most frail standing, Mercy chases us down and is renewed every morning.

> 2 Cor 9:8 KJV And God is able to make all grace abound toward you; that ye, always having all sufficiency in all things, may abound to every good work And God is able to make all grace abound toward you; that ye, always having all sufficiency in all things, may abound to every good work.

God sees us not as we are in the moment but as we are created and ordained to be. That is His Love in action. With the renewing of our minds, we begin to see what He sees and purpose our lives to line up with it. This disavows the enemy from placing our past front and center and prompting us to walk in uncorrected vision. We love God enough to make good on His redemption of our lives.

Evangelist Dorothy Norwood penned a song that said, "somebody prayed for me; had me on their mind, took the time and prayed for me!"

Realizing that God's love for us is intentional, unconditional, and unfailing, we are more apt to show that same love to others. Every human is a soul in need of God's salvation, whether his behavior indicates it or not. The spiritual battle for those souls has become very intense. As our tenure on earth draws steadily to a close, we are mandated to intervene for others for salvation, health, prosperity, and Kingdom citizenship. Through intercession, we can take the offensive in the spiritual battle, building up our family, community, nation, and world. When we take our place in the spiritual battle, God promises to "heal our land."

> 2 Chron. 7:14 (KJV) If my people, which are called by my name, shall humble themselves, and pray, and seek my face, and turn from their wicked ways; then will I hear from heaven, and will forgive their sin, and will heal their land.

Prayer

Sovereign God, thank you for this spiritual eye chart.
By faith and meditation of your Word, we also thank you
for correcting our vision. Thank you for reaffirming our
Kingdom purpose. Help us to trust your plan for our lives,
for you are the Creator, the author and finisher of our
faith, and the good Father who has plans of good
for those that are His.

Lord, daily help us to check our Love walk. We desire to
walk in pure, unselfish love because God is Love.
Let us not take those who cross our paths for granted and
recognize that we are both blessed and called to be a
blessing. Please season our words with grace.
Help us move from the seat of judgment to the suite of
compassion, prayer, and authority.

As our sight is transformed, help us to use it as the eagle does. Blessed with two sets of eyes, he uses what is natural to perform what is natural. But, when faced with a storm, he unveils the stronger set and faces the storm head-on.

Help us to understand that we are in a war against principalities and that you have equipped us with a stronger, spiritual set of eyes to help win the war.

Finally, Father, help us mature from admonishing others to see as we do, to the spiritual perfection of seeing as You see and loving as You love.

In Jesus' Name, Amen

Self-Reflection

*In my preface, I admonished each reader to read with
self-reflection and delve into the pages with the
intention of increasing your spiritual sight.*

*We have provided sections to journal your thoughts
and share what you have learned from the chapters of
"With My White Eye"*

Journal

Journal

Journal

Journal

Journal

Journal

Journal

Journal

Journal

Journal

Journal

Journal

Journal

Journal

Journal

Journal

Journal

About The Author

A native of Little Rock, Arkansas, and a descendant of generations of spiritual leaders, Reola B. Moore was once given the title "Quiet Storm" because of her soft delivery. Reola eased into her music ministry at the age of five, as her euphonious father created a platform and encouraged her to sing solos at church. Later, while serving as Minister of Music, she discovered a talent in music arrangement. At the age of twelve, she began teaching Sunday School, and of her several abilities, this gift is the most fluent. Moore has faithfully served in education, music, finance, evangelistic and administrative ministries. A prolific writer who has previously written skits, plays, and gospel lyrics has now followed the commission to pen her first book.

Living Water Books

The Christian Imprint Of

Butterfly Typeface Publishing

We specialize in Publishing, Marketing,

Graphics & Designs

Website: Livingwaterbooks.org

Living Water Books

John 7:38

He who believes in me, as the scripture has said,
Out of his heart will flow rivers of living water.

www.ingramcontent.com/pod-product-compliance
Lightning Source LLC
LaVergne TN
LVHW051154080426
835508LV00021B/2624